MW01146516

# Angry
# Children

..............................................................

Understanding and Helping
Your Child Regain Control

Michael R. Emlet

New
Growth
Press

newgrowthpress.com

New Growth Press, Greensboro, NC 27401
Copyright © 2008 by Michael R. Emlet. All rights reserved.
Published 2008

Cover Design: The DesignWorks Group, Nate Salciccioli and Jeff Miller, www.thedesignworksgroup.com

Typesetting: Robin Black, www.blackbirdcreative.biz

ISBN-10: 1-934885-26-6
ISBN-13: 978-1-934885-26-0

Library of Congress Cataloging-in-Publication Data

Emlet, Michael R.
  Angry children / Michael R. Emlet.
      p. cm.
  Includes bibliographical references and index.
  ISBN 978-1-934885-26-0 (1-934885-26-6)
  1. Child rearing—Religious aspects—Christianity. 2. Anger in children—Religious aspects—Christianity. I. Title.
  BV4529.E55 2008
  248.8'45—dc22

                                          2008011207

Printed in India
30 29 28 27 26 25 24 23    17 18 19 20 21

I f you have an angry child, you have undoubtedly experienced the emotional whirlwind that often emerges to leave relational, and sometimes physical, damage behind. You are most likely worn out, confused, and looking for answers to questions like:

- "How can I restore sanity to this chaos?"
- "How can I prevent these anger storms in my child?"
- "Why does this rage seem to explode out of nowhere?"
- "Will there ever be real peace in our home, or are bickering, quarreling, and fighting going to be the norm?"

Even as you read this, you may feel as though you are walking on eggshells, afraid that at any moment your child will erupt in anger over something minor.

When anger has become a pattern in your child's life, how can you help? You know that "man's anger does not bring about the righteous life that God desires"; but how can you minister to your child in such a way that he learns to be "quick to listen, slow to speak, and slow to become angry" (James 1:19–20)?

## What Is an "Angry Child"?

"Angry" is not necessarily the same as "strong-willed," although these categories do overlap. A child can be stubborn without being angry and aggressively defiant. Angry children go from zero to sixty when they hear the word "no" or when their desires are blocked. They have a very low frustration tolerance and easily blow up or explode. They throw tantrums consistently or display physical aggression to others. All children become angry, but these children are habitually oppositional and defiant and tend to bring chaos to family life.

## Where Does Anger Come From?

Like all of our emotions, anger does not come out of nowhere (although it sometimes seems like it does). Emotions don't just happen *to* your child; they are what your child *does* or *experiences* as an expression of his heart before God. In other words, our emotions are tied to our hearts, our inner nature that is living either for God or against God in every moment. What is in our hearts toward God directly affects our emotions, our words, and our actions. Notice what God says about the way our hearts are connected to everything we think, feel, say, or do:

- "The good man brings good things out of the good stored up in his heart, and the evil man brings evil things out of the evil stored up in his heart. For out of the overflow of his heart his mouth speaks" (Luke 6:45).
- "For out of the heart come evil thoughts, mur-

der, adultery, sexual immorality, theft, false testimony, slander" (Matthew 15:19).

- "The acts of the sinful nature [i.e. actions flowing from a heart set against God] are obvious: sexual immorality, impurity and debauchery; idolatry and witchcraft; hatred, discord, jealousy, fits of rage, selfish ambition, dissensions, factions and envy; drunkenness, orgies, and the like…" (Galatians 5:19–21).

- "You have heard that it was said to the people long ago, 'Do not murder, and anyone who murders will be subject to judgment.' But I tell you that anyone who is angry with his brother will be subject to judgment…" (Matthew 5:21–22). Notice that Jesus puts murder and anger in the same category—with the same punishment—because both issue from the heart.

The Bible's emphasis on the inward origin of anger suggests that helping angry children involves more than mere anger management techniques. To solve your child's anger problem, you must target the source of his anger: his heart.

Of course, not all anger is wrong. God's anger is holy, just, and loving, both in motive and expression. For Christians, it's appropriate and even necessary to experience anger about the injustices and sins that rightfully anger God. It's possible to experience anger and not sin (Psalm 4:4; Ephesians 4:26); but most likely, your child's anger is not honoring to God the majority of the time, either in its heart orientation ("I want what I want and you can't stop me") or its expression (tantrums, disrespectful speech, hitting).

Knowing that your child's anger comes from her heart should fill you with hope. Your child is not emotionally damaged and incapable of change. Jesus lived, died, and rose again so that all kinds of people—including children with very angry hearts—could be changed into people who love God and others.

## Take the Log Out of Your Own Eye

The Bible tells us that before you help others with their sins, you have to face and repent of your own sins (Matthew 7:3–5). When your child throws a tantrum or hits a sibling in anger, she is sinning against God and is responsible to him. But to stop there would be too simplistic. The Bible also acknowledges that we *can* provoke others to anger:

- "A gentle answer turns away wrath, but a harsh word stirs up anger" (Proverbs 15:1). Your response either stirs up anger in your child or defuses it.
- "Fathers, do not exasperate your children…" (Ephesians 6:4). This command assumes that there are things fathers (and mothers!) do that

frustrate and provoke their children, thereby creating an opportunity for their children to respond in anger.

Helping your angry child, therefore, must involve an honest assessment of your own contribution to the problem. You, as a parent, must search your own heart and evaluate whether your sinful attitudes, words, or actions stir up anger in your child. Ask yourself the following questions:

- Do I sometimes lose control when my child becomes angry?
- Do I and my spouse lose control with each other when we disagree?
- Do my expectations for my child vary from one day to the next?
- Do I discipline my child for something one day, and then fail to discipline her for the same thing another day?
- Do I apply different consequences to the same misbehavior?
- Do I communicate a consistent, low-level attitude of frustration with my child?

Until you honestly deal with your own sinful attitudes and actions, it will be difficult—if not impossible—to wisely, compassionately, and winsomely apply the gospel of Jesus Christ to your child's anger. As you learn to bring your sins to the cross, you will be able to help your child learn how to replace her angry lifestyle with one of repentance and faith.

Living with an angry child is tiring and emotionally draining. It's often hard to know what to do next and where to turn. But in the midst of your difficult circumstances, remember that you and your child are more alike than different. Both of you have particular temptations to sin; both of you desperately need the forgiveness of sins that Jesus provided for you on the cross; and both of you need the same power that raised Jesus from the dead in order to live in a new and peaceful way.

## Aim for the Heart

Since the child's heart is the source of his anger, helping him overcome anger involves targeting the root cause. It is likely that your child will resist seeing his temper originating from something wrong in his own heart. He will want to blame parents, siblings, or circumstances for his angry outbursts. But your child needs to learn that he is responsible for his anger. No one causes another person to sin (James 1:13–15). Outward behavioral eruptions are caused by inward (heart-based) cravings (James 1:14).

Your child needs to learn how his anger operates directly against God. Remember that the goal is not "nice" children who say "yes ma'am" and "no sir," but children who understand that they live under the ultimate authority of God. Too often parents only focus on the "horizontal" aspect of their child's sinful behavior—what the child has done to them. But targeting the heart helps your child understand that his attitudes, words, and actions violate God's standards first and foremost. This God-ward focus keeps the gospel front and center because sin against God and others has a remedy! If we confess our sins honestly, he is faithful and just to forgive us and cleanse us (1 John 1:9).

Targeting the heart also involves understanding the "whys" behind angry outbursts. It's not as simple as, "Well, he's a little sinner and he wants his own way!" That's a general truth about all human beings, but not particularly helpful in the moment. Rather, you need to uncover the particulars of your child's "own way." Ask God to guide you by his Spirit, so you will have the biblical wisdom to grasp what is really going on in your child's heart when he is angry. Then ask these questions:

- What specifically does my child desire, want, fear, or believe in this moment? Sinful anger reveals that some all-mastering desire is being frustrated.
- What specifically is my child not believing about God's character, actions, promises, and commands,

which would speak directly to his frustrated desires or fears?

The answers to these questions will help you learn how to craft a wise, heart-oriented response. You want to do more than externally control a child's anger through punishment, threats, rewards, or distractions. As your child grows to understand how his desires, fears, and beliefs fuel his destructive anger, you can point him to Jesus for specific help. He promises to pour out grace and mercy in your child's time of need.

What might this approach look like? Let's say your child throws a temper tantrum when asked to put away her toys at the end of the day. Using the above questions, what does she want in the moment? Perhaps she wants to do the next fun thing without delay. Perhaps she simply yearns for comfort and does not like the work involved. Perhaps she fears missing out on some other fun thing while she is completing this chore. What does she need to trust regarding God's revelation of himself in Scripture, which would speak to each of these areas of motivation and belief?

She needs to understand that God calls and equips her to live responsibly, and life is not principally about what is easiest for her, but what is most honoring to God and beneficial for others. Service to others is an honor that images Jesus (Philippians 2:1–11). She needs to see that picking up her toys, although it seems mundane, is one way she brings glory to the God of the universe (1 Corinthians 10:31). She needs to trust that God will withhold no good thing from her (Romans 8:32), so she is freed to engage in responsibilities that may not seem pleasant in the moment. She would be increasingly liberated to know that God meets her in her temptation toward unrighteous anger; he provides everything she needs in the moment to respond rightly (1 Corinthians 10:31; Hebrews 4:15–16). There are many other Bible passages that could speak at the level of her heart.

Finally, remember that shepherding the heart of your angry child is multifaceted; it involves the totality of life. We aim for the heart not only in the midst or aftermath of disobedience (as seen above), but in every interaction. If we only speak about the gospel in the midst of discipline, our children will view the gospel simply as the remedy for when they mess up. It certainly is that, but so much more! Aiming for the heart involves helping your child build a relationship with Jesus in the midst of all aspects of daily life, in fair weather *and* when the storms of anger are brewing.

## Understand the Wider Context of Your Child's Anger

Along with understanding the desires and motives of your child's heart, it is also very important to discern the potential physical and circumstantial factors that might contribute to your child's struggle with anger. While it is true that anger ultimately stems from the heart, it is crucial to ask what other contributing factors may be present. Considering the heart gives a *deeper* understanding of anger problems; considering the situational factors gives a *wider* understanding.[1] Understanding the wider context of your child's life will help you to be more patient, compassionate, and creative as you deal with him. Notice that discerning these various facets of your child's struggle requires wise, patient questioning and good listening.

Regarding potential physiological factors, research has demonstrated that some characteristics are typical of children who tend toward explosive anger:[2]

- Difficulties with short-term memory
- Decreased ability to organize and plan
- Difficulty with multi-tasking
- Being a "black and white" thinker (i.e. rigidity in problem solving—"There's only one way to do this," rather than flexibility—"There are several ways to approach this problem")
- Problems shifting quickly from one situation or set of expectations to another
- Difficulty in expressing oneself verbally
- Social skills weaknesses (e.g., difficulty recognizing

nonverbal cues; difficulty understanding how one is coming across to another person)

Notice that these potential weaknesses are not sin issues. They may *predispose* your child to respond in an angry, explosive way if he is challenged, but they are not sins in and of themselves. But when these weaknesses are present, the temptation increases for your child to become frustrated and lose control. How might the presence of some of these factors impact your approach?

For example, realizing that your child is hungry or tired will impact how you deal with him in the moment. Giving your child a banana rather than a "time out" may be the most appropriate response! It doesn't mean that you ignore defiance simply to avoid a fight. It doesn't mean that your child has an excuse for losing it. But it may mean forbearing (overlooking) the offense for the moment (Proverbs 19:11), and talking about it later when the child is well rested or fed. Or you may decide that the offense is serious enough to warrant intervention in the present despite the physical weakness (hunger) of the child. But you will do so with more compassion and patience, knowing the limitations your child faces.

Here's another scenario that you may face. When your child explodes in response to your request, "Please clean up your room before dinner," what's going on? While it's true that heart issues of laziness and love of comfort may be motivating the disobedience, have you considered that your child may also struggle to prioritize the mess, which may lead more quickly to frustration? Break the task into bite-size pieces: "First, pick up your shoes and put them in the closet. Okay, good. Now pick up your books and place them back on the shelves." Your child may still struggle to obey, but you have made appropriate allowance for his potential weaknesses.

Additionally, if your child doesn't seem to shift easily from one situation to another, plan accordingly. You may still require him to turn off the DVD player a few minutes before dinner, but giving ten-minute and five-minute warnings may go a long way in preventing a blowup when the time actually comes to press the "off" button.

Finally, if you learn that your child has been the victim of teasing or bullying at school, this too will factor into your overall approach to the anger that occurs at home after school. It doesn't excuse your child's anger toward you, but it does flesh out the broader contours of his struggle. God's grace always considers a suffering person's context even as it provides a remedy for sinful responses.

So, in order to minister with depth and breadth to your child, maximize your understanding of the various facets of your child's struggle—heart, body, circumstantial—and adjust your approach accordingly.

# Practical Strategies for Change

Focus on proactive relationship building with your child as opposed to problem solving in the moment. To use a medical analogy, a healthy diet and exercise are protective against heart disease. Doing those things may not fully protect a person against a heart attack, but diet and exercise may go a long way in preventing such a problem.

## Practical Ways to Build Your Relationship

*Look for ways to accentuate your child's strengths.* Don't focus so much on the weakness and sin that you can't see the ways God has uniquely gifted your child and is at work in his life.

*Look for opportunities to enjoy your difficult child.* Too often, the sum total of your interactions with your child can be negative. Or at the very least, the negative tends to swallow up the positive. Can you seek to create times of pure enjoyment? Do you show physical affection? Do you devote quantity time (not simply quality time) to playing with your child, engaging in what she wants to play? One mother realized that for years she had been too goal-oriented with her daughter. Their relationship radically improved when she invited her daughter for a walk several times a week with no agenda other than to enjoy time together. If your child does not believe that you love and enjoy her because you don't express it, you've got a strike against you when conflict brews.

*Examine the way you speak about your child to others.* Does it border on slander? Or do you season your conversation with thankfulness about the good you see God doing with your child? When you practice identifying the good in your child before others, it softens your own heart and positively affects your interactions with him.

*Look for ways to say yes to your child's request.* Too often we say no out of our own desire for convenience or comfort. God is a Father who lavishes good gifts on his children. His heart is not stingy. Romans 8:32 says, "He who did not spare his own Son, but gave him up for us all—how will he not also, along with him, graciously give us all things?" As an exercise this week, make a mental note of the balance between the times you say no to your child versus the times you say yes. You may be surprised—and convicted.

*Pray!* Intensity in prayer is a sign of humble dependence on God and hopefulness that God is and will be at work in the life of your child. Examine the content of your prayers for your angry child. Are they full of your own repentance? Are they more than "Give me some relief here"? Are they full of character-oriented petitions for your child, like praying specifically for the fruit of the Spirit in his life? Are you asking God to give you wisdom to address heart, body, and circumstantial aspects of your child's struggle?

## Model Consistency, Simplicity, and Dependency

### *Model Consistency*

- Model consistency in practicing what you preach. Be careful to treat your child with the same respect and care you want from her. If you habitually express the wrong kind of anger in your tone, words, or actions, your child will resent being held to standards you don't keep.

- Model consistency in expectations and rules. Decide on age-appropriate expectations for your child. If you don't know what they should be, ask a wise friend whose children are older than yours. Then be clear about what you expect from your child. Don't change your expectations from one day to another.

- Model consistency in discipline. You should have a plan for how you will respond to your child's misbehavior. Don't treat every offense of your child as a "10" on a scale of 1-10. When your child is out of control, it's easy to simply react and discipline out of frustration. When you do that, discipline is often punitive, not restorative.

### *Model Simplicity*
- Model simplicity by giving your child simple and clear instructions. Overloading her with instruction or explanation might precipitate a meltdown and will surely make a tantrum in progress worse. "When words are many, sin is not absent, but he who holds his tongue is wise" (Proverbs 10:19).

### *Model Dependency*
- Model dependency on God by repenting in front of your child when you haven't been consistent or simple. When you sin against your child, go to her and explicitly confess your sin (James 5:16). Ask her to pray for you, that God would help you to be a good parent. Let your child know that you are under God's authority also and want ultimately to please him.
- Model dependency by reminding your child that she must depend on God to help change her heart and behavior. Make sure that discipline not only involves identifying wrong heart motives

and behavior, but also involves asking Jesus for forgiveness and the grace to obey in the future (1 Corinthians 15:10).

## Develop Strategies for the Crisis Moment

So far, in developing an approach to the angry child, we have focused on admitting your own need for repentance; aiming to address your child's heart—his motivational desires and fears; studying the potential physical and situational triggers that provoke the heart; and building relationship constructively and proactively.

But what are the options when the storm clouds of anger are already brewing? What does it look like to address defiance while avoiding the meltdown? What should you do when you ask your child to pick up her toys and she refuses? You need to have a strategy for helping your child when she is tempted to lose control. Most parents only have two options in their response toolbox: sticking to their expectations for obedience no matter what (which usually leads to a tantrum) or dropping or reducing their expectations (which usually keeps the peace).

With the right parental motives (including an awareness of the primacy of the child's heart), either option may be a wise and godly choice. As mentioned earlier, dropping an expectation for a hungry child may well be the wisest option. But what other strategies might you use? Here are some you can add to your response toolbox:

*Pause.* Give your child time alone so she can regain self-control. This is not the same as a "time out," where you isolate a child for a set period of time as an act of discipline. Instead, this is a time for your child to calm down and reconsider her defiant attitude.[3] The pause can also help you to cool down and keep you from disciplining impulsively. This can be your time to think through your interaction with your child and pray to God for wisdom. When your child regains control, remember to affirm her. In the parable of the two sons (Matthew 21:28–32), notice how Jesus affirms the son who initially refused to obey but later did what his father asked.

*Use humor or laughter.* Sometimes a smile, a hug, or a tickle disarms your child, deescalates a brewing battle, and allows you and your child to regroup to address the issue at hand. Consider this a gentle response that turns away wrath (Proverbs 15:1).

*Cooperate creatively.* Work with your child to come up with a solution that takes both of your concerns seriously and is God-honoring and mutually acceptable (Philippians 2:4). Although this *can* work in the heat of the moment, it is better to do this proactively during a calm time, particularly if there are typical situations that set off your child's anger. What might this look like in practice?

Let's say a typical flash point for you and your son occurs about thirty minutes before dinner when he complains of hunger and asks for a snack. You don't permit a snack that close to dinner because you're afraid he will spoil his appetite. Creative cooperation begins with you and your child understanding each other's desires and concerns (Philippians 2:4). Your son's concern is hunger. Your concern is that he might spoil his appetite for the good meal you're preparing. Notice that neither desire is sinful. The next step is to work together to find a solution that addresses both concerns. This is critical because your typical solution ("You may not eat anything now") and your son's typical solution ("I want something to eat now") are completely at odds. What does a conversation that moves toward creative cooperation sound like?

> Parent (earlier in the day): "I've noticed that thirty minutes or so before dinner you usually want something to eat. What's up with that?"
>
> Child: "I'm getting really hungry by then."
>
> Parent: "So, because you're hungry, it's hard for you to wait the additional time until dinner?" *(This is an acknowledgement of your child's concern.)*
>
> Child: "Yes."
>
> Parent: "I'm concerned that if you eat something only thirty minutes before dinner,

you won't have room for a good meal. How could we work together to solve this problem in a way that honors God?" *(This is a critical moment. Here you are encouraging your child to be part of a mutual solution, rather than simply imposing a solution on him. This cooperative process is really designed to help your child grow in wisdom.)*

Child: "I don't know. Maybe if I just had a small handful of peanuts or something, instead of something bigger, I wouldn't spoil my appetite."

Parent: "Okay, that sounds reasonable. Let's see how it goes over the next week."

There are other ways to unite two concerns into one mutually acceptable solution that will avoid a typical battle. Some of them might be:

1. The child eats a snack as soon as he gets home from school;
2. Dinner is served earlier; or
3. The child eats a bigger lunch.

And there could be many more!

Of course, this is an easy case. Many other times it won't be that simple, and you will also have to proactively address the underlying heart issues that motivate defiance and anger. Even if your son is hungry, that doesn't give him license to fly into a rage. At the same time, working toward a mutually satisfying, God-honoring solution will go a long way to prevent future outbursts!

## Hang onto Hope

In conclusion, let me remind you of Paul's words in Romans 5:20: "Where sin increased, grace increased all the more." This is true for your child and for you. Failures will continue to occur, both in your child and in you. But when *you* are experiencing the renewing grace and forgiveness of Jesus in the midst of your parenting failures, you are emboldened to press on in ministry to your struggling son or daughter. And be assured of this: God will continue to pour out his grace, mercy, and wisdom as you seek him (Hebrews 4:15–16) so that you might be an instrument of redemption in the life of your angry child.

## Endnotes

1. I am indebted to David Powlison for this way of describing the relationship between the heart and physical/situational factors in the life of a child.
2. List adapted from Ross Green and J. Stuart Ablon, *Treating Explosive Kids: The Collaborative Problem-Solving Approach* (New York: Guilford Press, 2006), 18.
3. See Scott Turansky and Joanne Miller, *Good and Angry: Exchanging Frustration for Character...In You and Your Kids* (Colorado Springs, CO: Shaw Books, 2002), 67-69.